Just My Thoughts

by
Ed Loft

AuthorHouse™ UK Ltd.
500 Avebury Boulevard
Central Milton Keynes, MK9 2BE
www.authorhouse.co.uk
Phone: 08001974150

First published by AuthorHouse 5/18/2007

ISBN: 978-1-4343-0933-4 (sc)

Printed in the United States of America
Bloomington, Indiana

This book is printed on acid-free paper.

authorHOUSE®

Preface

There are many contributors, seen and unseen, to this book. My thanks to the roofers who left me seven tons of roof slates to move which took me three hours, with the rhythm of Longfellow's Hiawatha going round in my head, which became the poem "Power and Spirituality". I listened to it as though it was on a tape. I was spellbound, I would write parts down in the potting shed as I passed. After that poem six more appeared in a similar way. Then, when I realized it might not fade away, I listened for the lines that would link the poems together.

To Joanna, for her technical skills on the computer and being a patient sounding board, Chris for proofreading, Eric who printed an early draft and showed what it might look like.

Thanks to my sister, Jacqui, and her influences in making this possible. My friends in the Curiously Strong Art Group , Jen, David, Clare, Anna, Stuart, who were my models and Jayne who is at "The End" and is always a pleasure to draw. Penny, my other half, who gave me confidence with the first poem but then had the challenge of keeping me grounded the rest of the time. The unseen contributors are a law unto themselves but I thank them also.

Don't forget, thoughts are living things.

Ed

Introduction

How would a star view a celestial storm?

It is said that we are given what we need, not what we want. I think this applies to understanding also. We can use our dreams and imaginations, our meditations and inspirations to access as far as possible to discover our purpose. Others might say 'just do your bit and go'. Is the simple way best? Who would tell us? Would they tell us?

Someone near to me says that I think everything is about me. I say that is true. Likewise, everything is about them. I can only see from where I'm standing the cause and effect on the people around me. Everyone has responsibility for their thoughts (which I believe are living things) and their actions. The following pages are part of an ongoing journey that, in the right state of mind, it may be possible to glimpse an answer.

The Journey Begins

Just beyond my thoughts I can hear a melody, a young one's voice ... becoming clearer. He gazes at the petal in his hand thinking - how beautiful you are, how perfect you are, singing and chatting. Sing to me of how you see, the note is high and trill, the birds take over and all becomes one in the dawn chorus. Too precious a time, hold it within your spirit, a place of recognition and tranquillity. He laughs and says to me 'I am here, this is where I am'. I drift and see through his eyes. I feel all is for me, but I have only myself to give, nothing else is needed, my hand holds the petal and I listen to the song.

Dangling a foot in the stream, sitting on the soft heather, should I be lonely? This vast emptiness around me, the clouds changing shapes above me, to be lonely would imprison me where I sit. I hear the cries of the lonely, I put my hands in the stream and raise the clear water to the sun sending the flashing sunlight to the lonely ... I walk on.

I think of the sea, I think of the shore. I listen to the waves and become rested ... listen to the waves ....

> Listen to the waves aaashaaaaaaa
> Listen to the waves.
> Listen to the shale kreeeeeeee
> Listen to the shale.
> Listen to the trees shhhhhhhhhh
> Listen to the trees.
> Listen to the monks so low

They call the spirit to be with thee
To be amongst the waves aaashaaaa
To be amongst the trees.

She sang so high I could not reach.
He sang so low I could not see,
I asked them who they hopes to sound,
The Earth, they said, and also me.

Listen to the birds tralaaaaa,
Listen to the birds.
Listen to the wisping grass
The baying hedge
The pheasants' rasp,
Listen to the birds tralaaaaaa
Listen to the birds.

Listen to the silence ....

I saw a buzzard on a post, I thought ..... *perfection* ....then I saw another, all was still. I returned to the silence.

Time passed, scenery changing, smoke on the horizon, gunfire burning buildings, people shouting - chaos all around, adrenaline pumping, excitement, death or glory in young men's minds - death it is. 'Was my life wasted?' I hear him say. 'Help me', the soldier says. A piece of string near my foot, I hold it before me, straightening it from the centre, levelling the chaos around me, giving respite to those involved, the wailing quietens for a time. I move on accompanied by grief. A drone fills my being, a monk in saffron robes, an impossibly low drone telling me I'm not alone. I surround the grief with the vibration of the drone and think of our Creator giving comfort to the grieving. And of Power and spirituality.

With my clouded thoughts I ponder,
On the case of the Great Creator,
Who gave me soul that I might aspire,
To talk to spirit and be encouraged,
Ascend to heights beyond my imaginings,
To float in beauty, awe and wonder,
Gain access to the akashic record,
True ... False or just a flight of fancy,
Whilst I sip my gin and tonic,
Gazed on by one admirer,
Genes of old and notoriety,
Dictate the yearnings which must be quietened,
Sees beyond my wars and follies passing
And procreates the will of the masses
Genes directed from caves of the ancients.
Silently they lead us forward
Teasing, strength and beauty from mistake and longing
We only thinking it is our desire,
Our free will our right of passage.
It must be right but I cannot hear him
Did my genes tell me I could see him

Much have I to sit and ponder
Of the power and spirituality,
For there is the King
And there is the Queen
This one's the Jack of Spades
Which shall I be?
Which am I now?
Which was I long ago?
What of Bishop and the Knight!
Who ..? holds the 'Arc' by hand,
One of power the other of grace,
One of black the other of purple,
Send out dappled light into the darkness
For the pawns to acknowledge
Who is mighty?- cloth or sabre,
Giving power to non-believers
To rest and hope it all just passes
But no one can miss the Chalice
So reach out… and kiss the Father…
And hope there is light …. not darkness.

The fat old sheriff moves closer to the country band, he lifts his leg to the music, capturing the essence of the song and in so doing all music, something was achieved all wonders became one. I take the colour from the dance and offer it as enlightenment.

I move on. The sun is high in the sky. The skylarks hover and sing above the scrub earth of southern Spain, their song punctuated by the dull ring of the sheep's bells - more like cans than bells. The shepherd who is their leader sitting on a high point, indicating where the grass is with a stone. For a moment I enter his world.

He threw a stone and there they strayed
Trusting in his mournful gaze.
No purpose, drive or understanding,
which ones are safe in their surroundings.
No-one will notice me out here...
Who said that!?'
Sheep, shepherd or wild dog near?
I am small and ineffectual
Let me gaze upon the land,
Who is speaking?'
Sheep or shepherd?

Only you can understand.
Heat oppressing, mind regressing
Wild dog tip-toes near the band.
Scream out sheep for you're in danger!
Shepherd's dog lets out a growl.
Wild dog dead!
Sheep still grazing,
Shepherd throws another stone.

I turn away puzzling of my role in all of this, do I have one? Perhaps I'll never know, maybe, I should just accept what is before me, the closer to the material plane the more difficult to reason. A small baby has died. How should I think about this? A tragic loss, heartbroken parents, friends and relations ... a divine spirit experiencing the gateway of life, the trauma and torture of birth; maybe the final experiencing of a great spirit touching so many with the gesture of birth. The parents experiencing the miracle of life, albeit for only a short time, never to be forgotten leaving with them wonder and questions, to gain experience and maybe help someone else. I think of healing and why it might be possible, I raise the colours around me and meditate.

You could help!
You can you know.
Its within you, swirling round,
Faded blues, pinks and purples
Gold's, yellows and earthy browns.

I can do anything
My will is strong.
I'm almost chosen
To stand by the One.
I direct healing
And bring down the guards,
While all the time thinking
This isn't terribly hard.
Then some-one say Ego,
Another says Zen,
Is this really just so I can go to Heaven .. again.

Must change my thinking,
See who I am,
If some-one says help me,
Reply, I'll do what I can.
I'll point the direction
Like an old watering can,

Let the power flow through me
And pay it no mind.
To be there without Ego
Maybe helping just one
Knowing, not my will,
Just thy will, as always
Be done.

Its raining, maybe not everyone is here to learn, maybe some are here so that others can learn, maybe they are gifts untouchable by this plane - the soul trapped in the body that doesn't move or respond. The test is not theirs but ours, how do we respond to these 'unfortunates'. Accolade them and ask for enlightenment. The rain continues, I consider the age of the water and feel humble.

From my borrowed eyes, I watch our existence - a relationship of a son and a father, making sense to only them - how old is this story? I listen.

"So John said to me 'why don't you take your old man down the pub and get drunk?' Good idea, but I never did."

He waves and walks on by me
Some salute.. Returned gesture
Sparkling boots and gold braid glistening.
Even inmates are pleased to see him.
A man resigned to his duty,
Speaking only of respect unyielding,
Things passed down as pearls of wisdom,
Don't do this! And don't do that!
And how could you be the one uncaring,
Stand up straight son, set examples!
Don't be like your long-haired mates,
Hanging around doing nothing,
You'll end up inside with me.
Don't be mean Dad they're all good guys,
Don't judge them by their dirty jeans.
The fights and fogs that cloud our judgements,
Saying words that should never be,
Misunderstood, misunderstanding,
Begging for a cup of tea.
I'll show him its not all his way,
There is another path you see.
Years have gone and statures dwindle
Reinforcing remains the day,

Why is it always confrontation?
From now on it's only me.
Don't ask for consideration,
You're the one who made the rules.
All I want is recognition,
Gold and sparkle's no good for me.
Then one day I hear the message,
Not the first time told to me,
He has his tasks, yours are different,
No-one can do the other's d'you see.
All this time in wasted anger,
Instead why not just let it be.
Sitting by his bedside humble,
I love you Dad, Go in peace.

Detachment, I feel this is wrong,
but it is the only state that allows clear thought,
perhaps it is a luxury, maybe self indulgent,
it means that you don't take part - just observe,
even your own state.

If you recognise it and pass on observations
maybe it squares the circle.
I have to think more on this one.
The Earth plane, emotions driven to extremes,
tests and triggers observes being observed
maybe this is where emotions are experienced and indulged.

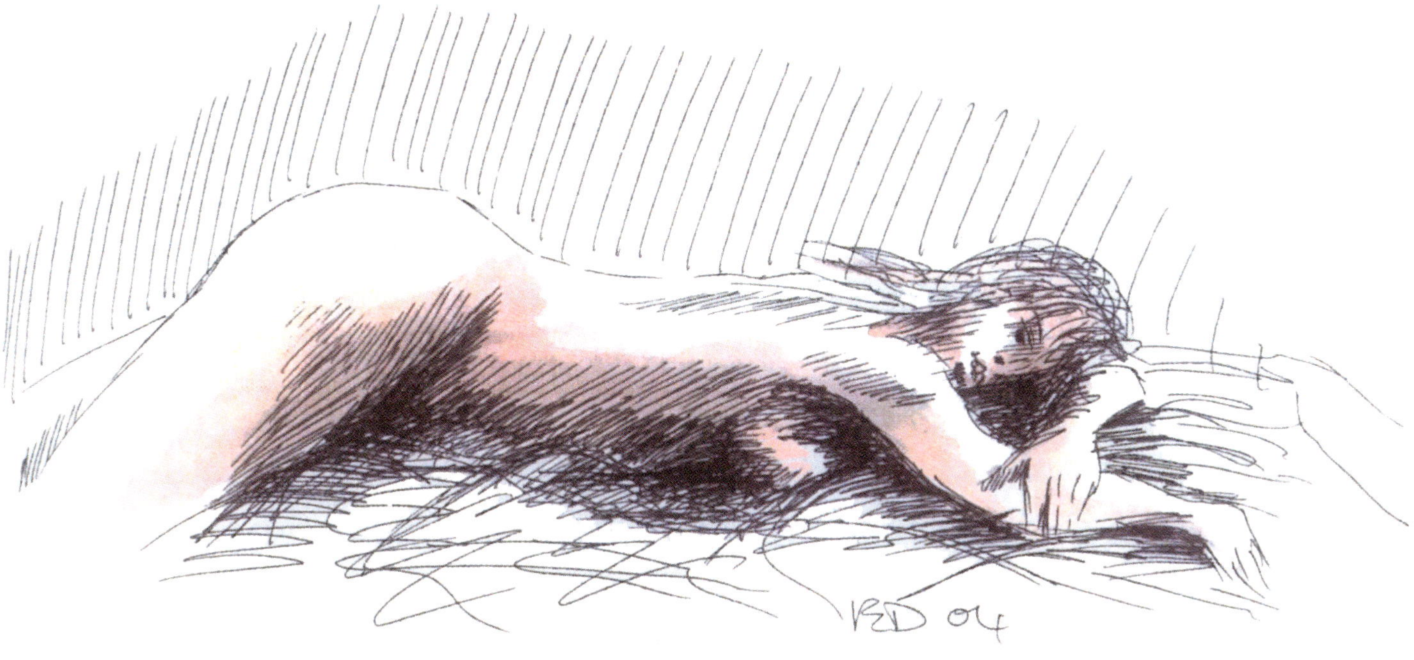

When he slipped his arm around her
Time stood still and all was quieter
Birds flew by, grasses tussled
Spiders ran and butterflies opened.
So hard the tree, so soft the grass
The choice of touch enhanced excitement.
Is this all for us this divine pleasure,
brought to us by our sponsors,
A gift from ourselves, unrecognised but not forgotten,
Forging links, reciprocating old presents.
So alone in their quarter with senses reeling,
Attracting hearts and courting gestures,
Pointing fingers and children's laughter
Old ones passing some perusing
And ones that bathe in love admiring,
Some so low with no progression,
Crouched in corners amidst obsessions,
And try to stand but stumble badly,
With blood soaked knees, distorted vision,
Some with sway and ease progression,
All goes on while lovers kiss.
A den so small that holds so many
But only two that see each other,
Touching fingers smiling eyes

Dwelling on the passing moment,
Thinking it will stay forever
Not knowing what has been achieved
Clarified thought regret or satisfaction,
Denied the trough between the wave
Assumed to be separate, not on going,

Part of us
Part of all
Only words,
Display,
Compete,
Deceive,
Contrive,
Delude,
Concede,
One touch ...
Just be.

The young one dances before me offering a flower.

I take it ..... I consider ....

The journey continues accompanied by a guide

You were an Eskimo. Was I?
You were a shepherd. Was I?
You were a Bishop. Was I?
You were a young German boy. Was I?
You were a Gladiator. Was I?

But the last occasion you dwelt on the Earth Plane was in the first Century.

What about the Eskimo? A shadowed life. But I was there! Sometimes you could watch him, is that not true? A shadowed life.

There was another...come, and watch with me...
"Black Feather...But how can we?"
"Just watch and listen..."

Black Feather glanced at the ragged man pushing the handcart down the street shouting 'two a penny, bring out your dead' merging with the fog of the old London Docks as he went.

The smell of his cargo bothered Black Feather he drifted back to when he was small, to the rotting corpse of a buffalo he had discovered at the foot of a sandstone cliff. He had squatted by it, pondering, it is dead, it was living, did the spirits know it was here? Had they looked the other way as it neared the edge of the cliff, too intent on grazing to notice the danger, or had it been left just to him to lament the passing of a great creature? He placed his hand on it acknowledging its life while searching the skies with his mind, saying: "Do you see it?"

"Ere, Josie, you'll never guess what I saw down the market today."

"Go on then, tell me, I know you'll never be able to keep it to yourself, George! Shout though, I can't hear for the girl crying."

"Well, there was this funny bloke you see, huge he was, make two of me...great big nose, and a feather in his hair, and eyes that you'd sooner he didn't look at you with."

"Sounds like a foreigner to me George, he'll wish he hadn't come with this plague, he'll be dead in a week like our little Violet, if she gets any worse."

"Don't say that dear, it breaks my heart! Half the neighbourhood's gone, what chance have we got? A pal of mine says he came off a Spanish ship that was raided by one of ours...good with herbs and potions, so the sailors took to him. Bit of a mean fighter by all accounts".

"Whatever he is, he's a long way from home."

"You're right there, Josie, I wonder if he can help our little Violet?"

"Dunno, George, but if you spot him again, ask him. What do they call him anyway?"

"Indian Joe's what they call him."

"So, go and find Indian Joe."

Black Feather lodged with the first mate whilst the ship was in for refit. He spent the days walking the streets south of the river observing the wretched state of the inhabitants. They must accept their fate like the goat in the bear trap, he thought.

"These are your people, Spirit!" he shouted.

"Concern yourself not!" replied the Spirit, the sound of his voice crushing Black Feather. Instinctively, he reached out placing his hand on a wall earthing himself, drawing on the timeless energy of the stone as he reeled.

Black Feather felt an arm around him... "You' all right, mate?" said George.

"Sometimes when you shout they hear you." said Black Feather.

"Tell me about it." said George "I think it's best to keep quiet myself. Bit of a funny turn was it... thought maybe the plague was getting to you?"

"Yes." Black Feather grunted.

"Don't worry", said George "the Almighty is watching over us."

"Yes." said Black Feather "the Great One is watching over us. Thank you, little man."

"Come and have a drink", said George. "My place is not far from here."

Black Feather went with him looking back at the river where a crimson glow laid on the water.

"It's a bad time for us" said George "Not knowing who's going to be next. And you, a stranger, walking straight into it. You should have turned tail and run as soon as you got here."

Black Feather said the plague had arrived as they did and now they couldn't leave, so now he will do what he can. Black Feather had been gifted as a linguist and spoke many tribal tongues. The European languages were a puzzle to him, but not impossible... discovering long ago that people always spoke about the same things, just in different terms.

They arrived at George's house where Josie was wiping the sweat from little Violet's forehead. She gasped as Black Feather entered the room behind George.

"Don't be scared." said George "This is Indian Joe."

Josie looked into Black Feather's eyes and said, "You can help my little girl … can't you?"

Black Feather said nothing. She stayed staring at him and realized that as she looked there were no sounds around her. She felt warm and light and there was a blue glow in the room. She knelt down beside Violet's bed, comforting her, transferring the peace she felt to Violet who opened her eyes and smiled at her.

Black Feather asked George for a bowl with some warm water in it. Taking a leather pouch from his jacket he mixed the herbs in the bowl. He knelt down too, letting the vapors from the mixture waft over little Violet, whose breathing became deeper and she drifted off to sleep.

"Will she die?" asked George.

"No." said Josie as she turned to look at Black Feather.

"I will ask that this one stays" Black Feather said and left.

"Spirit of the red glow, I would speak with you!" Black Feather shouted onto the river. The mist stirred, again Black Feather began to shout - the mist engulfed him, chilling him to the bone.

“Feel my power.” said the Spirit. Black Feather sank to his knees.

“Great One.” said Black Feather “Why do you choose Evil?”

“Evil, you say Sha Ha Waa De.” (the Spirit addressed Black Feather by his true name) “Good and evil are one, you should know this Sha Ha Waa De.”

“But you make these people suffer, that is Evil.”

“To purify the spirit - remember your Sun Dance. Was your pain evil - or was it glorious? Remember what you saw, who you spoke to, what you learned!”

Black Feather wept as he remembered the visions, so beautiful and serene; the sudden understanding of intricate messages passed on to him by unseen ancients; to understand he was not alone.

“Spirit.” said Black Feather “Give life to the child. I ask for them not for me.”

“It is done”, replied the Spirit “Like the buffalo that was glorified in heaven - because you asked.

> Thank you for reminding me of Black Feather, his trials were great and his tasks daunting, but he was always open to Spirit.
>
> My journey is still taking place … Thanks you, old friend, for our conversation.

The Journey Continues

How do we learn? Is it possible to listen without Ego, therefore not judging, but acknowledging the lesson no matter where it comes from? On a building site as a young man we dug footings with spades no mechanical diggers then where I lived, I said to the older man next to me, I can't make any impression here, keep doing what you're doing was his reply, a lesson acknowledged and at times still pertinent today.

These poems and sketches are attempts at capturing the essence of a situation, perhaps for a particular instance the whole panorama is unveiled and so becomes the illustration of that moment. If that moment is while dreaming or everyday living by acknowledging its message a lesson can be learnt and progress made, allowing the search to go on. If you ask for guidance in your search it will be given.

A Gardening Query

Who owns the spaces between the flowers?
The shady places to dwell for hours
The mice to run, the birds to gather.
Or fairies just to sit and chatter.

Who owns these spaces that expand whilst looking?
A treasured gap for a careful footing,
Somewhere to lean, a cranefly gestures.
Spreading wings of silk-like textures.

Who owns these mystic missed out plantings?
That existed ere the fountains.
Do they make a maze or labyrinth?
That tempts you to chance upon their mysteries,
Of spaces gathered round about him.

Like children listening to a story.
Entranced in visions great and worldly.
The answers not unfolding lightly.
Disgust and tortured hair-pulled hours.
Who owns the spaces between the flowers?

Still thinking

Thoughts, dreams, poetic themes,
Thoughts of shape, line, evocative times.
Once a thought is out, and gone.
What lies in wait..?
Another one!

The None Entertaining of Cold Cotes

<u>Guest:</u>

At last! she said we've come to rest,
Oh tea! My thanks that cakes' the best,
What views, what peace, what winsome weather
What funny ponies that stand together!
Such space, such undulating hills,
And mists that under plant the trees.

<u>Cold Cotes:</u>

Shceeeeeee whaaaaaaaaa shceeeeeeee
Craaaaaak craaaaaak ....
Flaaaaa flaaaaa flaaaaa trrruttttttttttttt
Scrut...scrut scrut scrut chr che chr
Buthaaa buthaaa buthaaa buthaaa

<u>Guest:</u>

Was that my heart? That subdued sound!
These walls don't speak to me of now!
I'm not known, but yet I am,
These rocks, this stone, these precious sands!
Within these walls of glass I'm seen,
from here to all eternity.

Cold Cotes:

Beeeee Braaaaaaveee beeee stiiiiiillll
Beeeee liiissstttteeenniiiing wweeellll
Tooo yooouuurr hheeaaaaarrtttt
Thaaaattt beeeeaaaattttsss sssoooo weeeell
Bbee truuuee ttoo yoouuur uunnteetherd wiill.
That brought you by your destiny.

Guest:

To dwell was all I wished for long,
The urgency of life atone,
Within these aged walls serene,
Remain here for a while unseen,
And judge the play or be the judged,
Of life and loves' lament extreme.

Cold Cotes:

Be still, be calm, be rested well,
For this, is the only place to dwell,
At peace and rare tranquility,
Of illusion or reality…

Diana's Garden Poem

What's your name? You long and squiggly,
Sneaking up on me…you wriggly,
Is it out the rain you're wanting?
Puddles...Ocean deep most daunting.

What's your name? You darting flutterer,
Flashing red and brown…you chatterer,
Peep, peep, peep then gone…oh! There you are!
Hiding in the hedge full of, caterpillar!

What's your name? you small and fury,
You're tunneling under the flowers too early!
That twitching nose and hands doing paddling,
Heaping soil tripping all not noticing.

What're your names? You Fairies gathering,
Laughing, dancing, chasing, meandering,
Making out that all we believe…we could!
Then live with Diana…Giggling, in the wood.

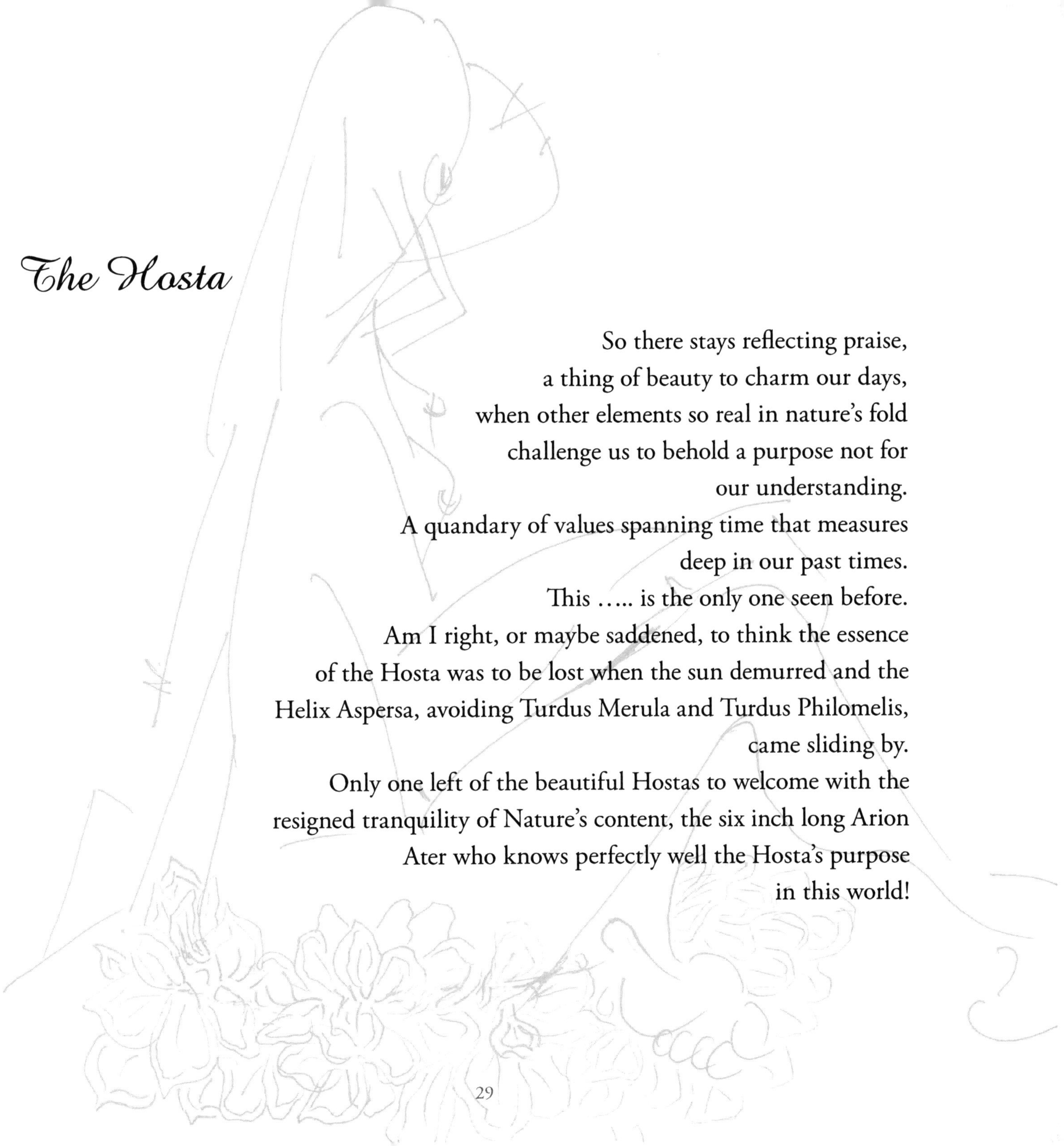

The Hosta

So there stays reflecting praise,
a thing of beauty to charm our days,
when other elements so real in nature's fold
challenge us to behold a purpose not for
our understanding.
A quandary of values spanning time that measures
deep in our past times.
This ….. is the only one seen before.
Am I right, or maybe saddened, to think the essence
of the Hosta was to be lost when the sun demurred and the
Helix Aspersa, avoiding Turdus Merula and Turdus Philomelis,
came sliding by.
Only one left of the beautiful Hostas to welcome with the
resigned tranquility of Nature's content, the six inch long Arion
Ater who knows perfectly well the Hosta's purpose
in this world!

Hmmm, a Seat!

Green… the hunting Praying Mantis,
Coloured by the background floorless,
Still the structure proud and blameless,
Steadfast in its purpose shameless,
Comes along the victims shadow,
Changing tones and stirring odours,
Giving cues to hunters waiting,
Hydraulics pumped electrics charging,
Passed the point of no returning,
Till the touch of life adjourning.

Black… the serpent smooth and silent,
Scenting air while searching shading,
Hissing out the welcome presence,
While careless footfalls near evading,
Hidden under wooden ramparts,
Withdrawn from darting nervous eyes,
Waiting for a chance to impart,
The deftly skill that will arise.

Bright… the bird that perches singing,
And the breeze so gently chilling,
Cools the ground that longs for weeping,
Also carries her song afar,
To waiting ears and dreams unfolding,
Come…the waiting point to greet,
Sky of gold and light forgoing,
For all the world in search….a seat.

Why This Seat?

Why this seat?
Why here?
Why this time?
Which has priority?
I turn to my left and the moment is passed,
The seat is the only constant,
What brought me here?
How many years did it take?
58… plus the age of the earth,
To choose a seat?

Why this seat?
Perhaps it was not the seat but the place itself,
The seat occupies the space where I want to be,
So why not sit on it!
Is this the bottom of a vortex?
A doorway where dimensions can be crossed?
If I sit on the seat and look at my hand,
Can I see through it?

Is this seat where the best feeling is?
Do I need to look be hind me?
Or do I know what is there without looking?
If so….It is the right seat!

"Some't Like"

This is the tale of some't like
Who couldn't read and couldn't write
And couldn't tarry with the shows
Not catching on to looks and flows

Instead he dwelt with fury friends
That nestled to him come what may
And walked beside him discussing all
Truly gratifying in the thrall
Of making sense of all the ends

While taking on the chores of life
Each one a task to be done just right
Not thinking why, or if, or might
So all is balanced and even by night
And in the dawn the sun so bright
Knowing it was some't like.

Thank you

I would like to thank the birds for ignoring me,
For flapping their wings and doing their thing
And standing on one leg and catching a bee,
Yes! I'd like to thank the birds for ignoring me.

I would like to thank the moles for ignoring me,
For digging holes and eating worms
And poking their heads up not in the leased bit concerned,
And putting waves in the lawn just like the sea,
Yes! I'd like to thank the moles for ignoring me.

I would like to thank the spiders for ignoring me,
The none thinking spiders that fashion the webs,
The none thinking spiders that stalk their pray,
The none thinking spiders that commit hari-kari,
Yes! I'd like to thank the spiders for ignoring me.

I would like to thank the weather for ignoring me,
You know how it goes, too hot, too cold, too wet, too dry,
It's surprising that the weather's not charging a fee,
Yes I'd like to thank the weather for ignoring me

I would like to thank my spouse for ignoring me,
Yes! I'd like to thank my spouse for ignoring me,
While I sit under a tree drinking a beer,
With a bird near my head, singing tral-lee,
A mole at my feet eating his tea,
The sun on my back… and a none thinking spider there on my knee,
Yes! I'd like to thank my spouse for ignoring me…

The Request

Pray for me…

He said… like someone with no recollection of past events, forgetting that he brought things with him.

Pray for me…

Is this weakness? What is strength? To shout out " here I am," supposing nobody comes, what then?

Pray for me…

Why so desperate? so urgent, have you forgotten already the meetings you had, the plans that were made, the great tasks to be done!

Pray for me…

Is your faith so fragile that you crumble at the eve, not knowing where you stand or the place you occupy.

Pray for me…

To ask is recognition take your strength from that, don't be lost in the downward spiral of self-pity and ego, your body is a vehicle not the destination.

Pray for me…

My mind is not my own, he said.. I am in turmoil, desperation, frustration my values have gone, I am wasted, exhausted.

Pray for me...

Are you only helped if you understand all things? What about those with no understanding or ability to understand, are we saying " if I can't see it or don't know about it, it can't exist", you only need one dream to know this isn't true.

Pray for me...

The request goes on, is it reassurance that is needed? That you matter enough to be prayed for, is the request through ego, or are we literally the " children of God" craving reassurance like a child.

Pray for me..........

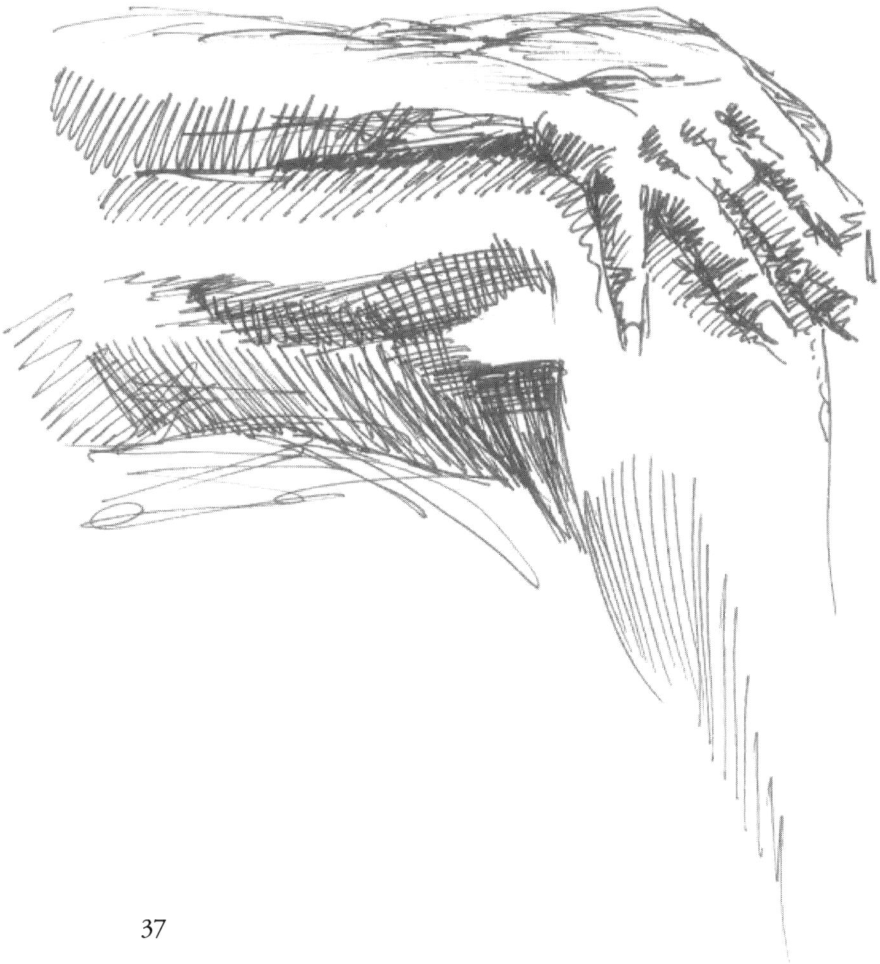

The Ballad of the Hanging Tree

Once upon a sunlit Tuesday,
Marco played at being tutor.
His mother shouting be a good boy,
Plant this acorn for the future.
Marco laughed at the presumption,
That this acorn could guide his future,
But just to please his mother smiling,
Raced to the hilltop shouting wildly.
Here I'll plant it bold and forthright,
Not seeing the old lady passing,
Muttering oaths and limping strangely.
Grabbing his hand she whispered lowly,
That tree will be your death… unholy.
Ah! Away from me you old and moldy,
Its mine to plant, and no other!
For its bows to shade my lover.
Marco hoping this would shock her,
But on she went till under cover,
Of the lowland trees that offered shelter,
From grey clouds gathering about her.
Hah! said Marco shrugging shoulders,
I'll plant it over near that boulder,
That will protect it from the wind,
Feasting birds and slimy things.
Feeling happy at the concept,
Of this tree a boyhood marker,
Then tall and strong as in his manhood.
Uncompromising in its stature,
Proudly back to mothers cooking,
Satisfied with all his plotting.
Onward… onward… gained momentum,
Living… feeling… no exemptions.
Till there she stood, a gasp... yes soundless.
Perfection, owning love that's boundless,
Protective all but tunneled vision,
Possessions naught but games oblivion.
No reasoning will or chance to fight her,
Just overwhelming love despite her.
Did she fondly look upon him?
Differently to others wooing,
Some say yes and some say… well..
And some say she is his today.
However now this young boy teasers,
Stood before him... "Mona Lisa".
The fire he felt was encompassing,
Friends told him it wouldn't be lasting,
But for him it was unimaginable,
To be parted from his love so joyful.
Ten years on no fading pleasure,
But for Charles… who came by calling.
And entertained… while one out working,
Reclaiming just her lusty pastimes,

While Marco trusting all around him.
Discovered there was more to dealing,
Than earning bread and buying flowers
The tranquil person friends had called him,
Slow to rise to bate before him.
And Charles the well connected son,
To important people of the town.
Who made play and joked thereafter,
The conquistador of hearts left wanting.
Toasted by his friends around him.
No mercy given to Marco's feelings,
Or second thought to him now kneeling,
The bar room loud with heraldic laughter.
While Marco sank beyond all reasoning,
One table offering stoic barricade,
A moments pause… before cascade
Of leaping man with both Knives drawn,
Then falling friends and screaming victims,
And Charles before him white as sheeting,
Saying nothing but open mouthed.
With each knife embedded in his person,
Could only drop his head… and die.
Marco ran, the town up chasing,
Over locks and fields ran he,
Till surrounded… high the viewpoint,
To the tree that stood there guarding,
Then captured Marco, beat him senseless,
Laid him on the boulder helpless,
Drawn up to the bow now shading,
And Marco recognizing all.
Cried out… that love was all he lived for,
But the mob hauled tight the tow,
With his last breath he said… forgive them!
Then came the sound of breaking bow,
But no release from death was given,
Only stillness… Of the Now…

the end

Printed in the United States
91104LV00001B